Where There Is No Comfort
Seven Days in Ethiopia

Juliann Troi

Eloquent Books

Eloquent Books
An imprint of Strategic Book Group
P.O. Box 333
Durham CT 06422
www.StrategicBookGroup.com

ISBN: 978-1-60860-753-2

Printed in the United States of America

Book Design: Stacie Tingen

For Pat who gave me wings to fly
and never doubted I could soar with eagles.

Home?

I rise slowly to wakefulness, sensing darkness, feeling confused. The bed beneath me feels different, fuller, and more luxuriant. My mind tells me I should be comfortable but I'm not. The downy thickness of the comforter that covers me can't completely ward off a chill. Why is it so cold? Ethiopia is not so cold. Yet I am no longer in Ethiopia. Am I?

I strain my ears, listening for the hyenas yipping bark but hear only a cold March rain against the skylight in the bathroom. *I think of the rain, of how the rains have not come this year as they were supposed to. No rain promises drought, and with drought comes famine—certain death for millions in a country in which the livelihood of 90 percent of the population is subsistence farming.*

Still fresh is the memory of how, on the last day of the clinic, we ran dangerously low on bottled water, and I knew the creeping prickle of the fear the Ethiopian people constantly live with. Without clean water we would perish quickly, the vast extent of our American wealth and privilege of no use to us. Never will it be "just water" to me again.

I lie perfectly still struggling to make sense of things. *Am I not in my narrow bed at the Heme, Hossana's idea of a five-star stay, the crowning achievement of an ambitious family that, here in the States, wouldn't likely pass code or a health department inspection?*

Any minute now, bright light from the hall will come flooding through the pane of glass above the door as Maki, the hotel's very able manager, turns on the hall light. Soon the now-familiar Islamic morning chants will be cast over Hossana by loud speaker from the town's mosque.

I wait in eager anticipation for what has become a daily routine to begin. I feel a trill of excitement as I contemplate the coming day. My excitement evaporates. For me, it is back to being wife and mother in my comfortable suburban home but for them . . .

For them the day holds hard work with little return save subsistence, a life of toil for life's sake.

I have come to appreciate as never before what a precious gift is life. Yet life, the continuance of it, is so tenuous and fragile in much of Ethiopia. Today is more than enough to bear, tomorrow a burden too heavy to shoulder. Yet every night they are relieved of the load of yesterday and weighed down afresh as tomorrow becomes today, over and over until all their todays are used up. Amazingly, the Ethiopian people seem satisfied with the exchange.

And for me? What is there now for me? For me there is only the darkness and the rain.

Still battling confusion, I sit up and swing my legs over the edge of the bed. I frown down at my pajama-covered legs, fingering the light green cotton. I didn't take these with me so I must be . . .

Home? My eyes sweep the room. I can make out the dark outlines of familiar objects lining the walls but it is my dog's soft, inquiring tongue across my dangling foot that finally clears the fog. Yes, I am home.

I glance at the nightstand to my right. Neon orange tells me it's just past 2:00 a.m. So early. Not in my world that was, though. It is nine hours later there, nearly noon, the time for all activity at the clinic to cease as the Ethiopians drop everything and break for lunch.

Knowing sleep will not be coming again soon I decide not to fight it. So I begin the impossible task of trying to meld back into the world as I used to know it, pretending I'm not forever changed.

Can one see the things I've seen over the last week and not be altered somehow? We hear cold and informational statistics all the time. But there is a very real, very human factor the statistics can't effectively capture—the suffering of those trapped within the numbers.

I discovered that this human factor can be a two-edged sword. While there is no worse nightmare than holding a starving child nearing death, there is no greater high than walking away from a desperate situation knowing you made a real difference and changed circumstances for the better. You saved a life.

It was through the latter that I came to appreciate the expressiveness of the Ethiopian face. Their smiles seem brighter and more genuine, like the sun after a devastating storm, fiercely battling adversity to appear.

***

As I shuffle through a dark, quiet house I can't help but feel that my world has taken a strange turn. A grim smile is all I can manage for the trip now gone by, the adventure of a lifetime to the most thrilling and challenging of places.

Saturday . . .

The florescent light that assaults my eyes as I flip on the kitchen light reminds me of the Ethiopian sun that seared my skin and eyes from the first moment I stepped into it from the airport terminal, finally reaching our destination after some harrowing delays and difficulties.

Thanks to an ice storm that grounded us for most of the day in the St. Louis airport at the outset of the trip, I had a good opportunity to become acquainted with my "mission buddies," the folks I would be doing life with for the next ten days. Unfortunately, it caused our eighteen member group to miss connecting flights in Chicago and Frankfurt.

The original plan was that we would arrive Friday evening and stay the first night at the luxurious Hilton in Addis Ababa, then proceed down-country to the town of Hossana the next morning. Instead, we landed about the time we were supposed to leave for Hossana.

Travel weary and grateful to be on the ground again, we expected to be met by the shuttle buses that were hired to ferry us around for the week but found no one there. A call informed us they would be along in fifteen minutes.

More than an hour later we were still cooling our heels in the airport parking lot. As with the delay in St. Louis, I used the time to get acquainted—this time with Ethiopia.

The airport was situated to one side of a bowl, abutting the hills that ring the capital city. But from where I lounged against my luggage getting the first sunburn of the trip I couldn't see that much city and, though it was a clear and sunny morning, the hills were largely hidden by a gray-brown haze.

The acrid bite of something strangely pungent and vaguely familiar hung heavy in the air. It hinted of burning vegetation, and something else that dredged up bad memories of cutting through lesser-used high school stairwells and finding the "potheads" scoring hits between classes. I later learned that in Ethiopia hemp is the fuel of choice for cook fires.

Tropical bushes and trees were scattered about the area, their glorious fuchsia blooms standing boldly against a rather drab backdrop of corrugated tin and glass.

I decided that urban Ethiopia, at least around the airport, tended toward something of a tropical paradise meets warehouse district. It left me wondering what I had gotten myself into. So far it hadn't been what I expected at all.

At long last two shuttle buses arrived and we were on our way. I discovered that I was on the "party bus" when one member of the Ethiopian medical staff we called Benny, stood up and started leading the other Ethiopians in song. That is how they wiled away the 160 mile trip south.

At one point, Benny invited me to sing something we sing in our churches and I obliged, but my feeble attempt seemed somehow lacking and empty compared to the soulful liveliness of Ethiopian praise music.

At a halfway point, we stopped at a hotel/restaurant for a meal and to meet up with Pat Bradley, President of International Crisis Aid. Unfortunately, by this time I was exhausted and completely overwhelmed by the newness of it all. To say I wasn't hungry is a gross understatement. In fact, it was all I could do to keep from throwing up and dissolving into hysterical tears.

What am I doing here?

The question kept running through my mind like a mantra as I leaned against the railing of the second story stoop outside the restaurant, encased in a cocoon of misery. It was only four hours into the first day of a seven day mission and I had already defined and redefined discomfort a dozen times over since leaving home three days before. I was certain I had reached the very edge of my world, butting against the physical and emotional limits of my endurance. Little did I realize; this truly was just the beginning of what would turn out to be the most amazing adventure of my life to date.

***

I drink in the peace as I recline in my living room, sipping the coffee I have made and my gaze travels the pristine cream colored walls, broken only by the vivid oils capturing scenes of the Wild West; a rugged period in American history no longer so impossible for me to conceive.

Suddenly, the textured cream seems to morph and become bare mustard yellow plaster. I am again in the home Pat and his team took me to the first night in Hossana, the home of a family ICA has been helping.

It was fully dark when we stepped outside the gates of the Heme for the short hike up the steep rock and dirt street. To my surprise there were still dozens of children swarming about us as we made our way to a squat mud brick and tin building at the end of the block.

We were greeted at the gate of the dwelling by still more children and ushered into a pitch black courtyard. Because I am night blind, I sensed more than saw walls to the left and in front of me. To the right, a thin beam of light from a single naked bulb interposed upon the darkness.

With mixed feelings, I followed Pat toward the light and was greeted by Esther, a woman most certainly younger than my forty-three years but looking eons older. She shook my hand and mumbled words I could not understand as she extended a traditional Ethiopian greeting: a kiss on the left cheek, on the right and again on the left.

Once in the small, rectangular room this family called home, the first thing I noticed were surprisingly colorful red and blue rugs, overlapped to completely cover the floor. As we were seated in straight-backed wooden chairs lining three of the walls, Pat observed, in an aside to me, that there was usually a bed in this room. He went on to share that this single mother of five has done well enough in her bread-making business to rent another room across the small courtyard.

While he and the other members of the team exchanged customary pleasantries with Esther, making inquiries about the weather, the family, her health and the health of her children, I covertly studied the windowless room. It was still quite stuffy from the day's heat and there were alarmingly large cracks in the plaster covering the gray block walls.

In the corner along the short wall at the end farthest from the door, there was a tall, square table spread in modestly magnificent fashion. Atop a bright cloth were set scratched and scarred bottles of Pepsi and Fanta orange soda, napkins, and a huge woven bowl full of popcorn which we were shortly offered.

Sarah, Esther's outgoing eleven-year-old daughter, who was seated next to Pat, squirmed excitedly in her chair. She is the one he has come to see. Crystal-blue eyes dancing with delight as he gave the girl a hug, he asked how school was going. Pulling out the achievement medal she had recently won, she proudly reported that she is doing very well. He asked if she would like to go with us to the clinic in Angacha the next day. She had no answer for she needed her mother's permission but it was obvious she really wanted to go.

Pat turned his attention back to Esther who had seated herself on a low stool across the room. Behind her was a darkly cavernous portal that would have been the opposite short wall were it not the entrance to another room. That one has not been rented so it is given over to clutter rather than the family's use.

On the floor in front of her was a small charcoal-filled brazier and a modestly decorated black decanter, which I soon learned was an Ethiopian coffee pot. The pot was unlike any I had ever seen before with its bulbous bottom, tall, thin neck, short spout, and pointed lid. There was a certain exotic elegance about it that stood in sharp contrast to the shabby simplicity of the surroundings.

After settling the pot on the glowing coals, Esther attempted to corral her youngest, a restless toddler, and answer Pat's questions but struggled with both. Although her children have learned English, she has not, so a member of the team was sent back to the Heme in search of a translator.

While we waited, making small talk with Sarah and her older brother Haptum, an old man in decorous skull cap and dirty-white linen robes shuffled into the room to take a seat in the corner to Esther's right. She introduced him as her uncle. He had apparently come to chaperone the visit.

Shortly our translator arrived. No, Esther was not comfortable letting her daughter go with us to Angacha, but quickly added how grateful she is for all that Pat has done for her family.

Our attention was directed to the center of the room, where on a second, smaller table, was placed a very large cake of yellow bread, perhaps two feet by two feet. Since Pat was the honored guest he was requested to cut it. He sawed free an obligatory piece or two before gratefully turning the task over to his wife, Sue. Once she had carved out a dozen or so squares, one of the other children put them in a basket and passed it about the room.

As we concluded our visit Esther told us that they would soon be relocating. She has been informed that this house, along with the other buildings on this block, are slated for demolition to make room for another hotel. Now that the newly paved highway has come to Hossana there is more business and more need for rooms. She did not know where they will go yet.

Apparently, this is not the first time she has faced such a dilemma. A year or two before, Esther owned a bread shop across the street until it was bulldozed in favor of something else, so she lost her place of business. Likewise, she will soon lose her home. I thought it strange that no one seemed overly distressed about it until I was told that in the Ethiopian economy "soon" can mean years.

So goes life in Ethiopia, a land where nothing is certain.

Waiting in the airport parking lot in Addis Ababa for our transportation to arrive.

Half-way point where we had our first meal in-country and met up with Pat Bradley and his team.

Typical rural homestead. We passed many on the way to Hossana.

A view of the Heme from the front courtyard

One of the streets that ran by the Heme.

Another street adjacent to the Heme with partial view of the backyard mound and houses I looked into.

The adoring masses of children greeting Pat after he returns from a long day in the field.

A little market in Hossana

Playing a game with the kids in the street in front of the Heme.

Where Esther and her family live just up the street from the Heme.

Typical sights along Hossana's streets.

A homestead next to the new highway.

A vulture in the tree on the mound in the Heme's backyard.

The tower of the local mosque can be seen in the distance.

Even with the new highway the old ways of transporting goods are still the favorite.

Sunday . . .

I prop my chin in my hand trying to concentrate on the Bible in front of me but, despite the coffee I have consumed, my exhausted mind refuses to focus. I don't feel much different on this, my first full day home, than I did the morning of my first full day in Ethiopia. It was a Sunday.

I woke that morning with the light from the hall after a fitful night's sleep feeling ready for the day. Although it was still very early, I rose to face it.

The sun had not risen yet and the morning was cool, in the 50s. After the frigid temperatures of the winter months in the States it was a drastic improvement to my mind, but Maki, the Heme's manager, bundled up in hat, scarf and gloves, declared it freezing.

I wanted to go outside and enjoy the morning. However, Maki informed me that I was not allowed to go outside just yet so I took a seat on the couch in the foyer outside the little restaurant at the end of my floor. Two other ladies from my group had risen as well so I had company while I waited for breakfast. Conversation was light and pleasant still the wait seemed interminable. I was eager to see Hossana and get my bearings.

Finally, at 7:00 a.m. I was released to go downstairs to a large dining room reserved for our group at the back of the hotel.

As I went out the back door of the first floor and down a flight of stairs, I got my first look at the Heme's back yard. Most of it was taken up by an enormous two-story dirt mound covered with scrubby brown grass. There was a scraggly tree or two at the top and a speckled goat staked at the bottom. The vultures camped out in the branches of the trees looking down on the goat somehow made the scene complete, like something from a Far Side cartoon.

I had no idea of the mound's purpose, for it seemed completely out of place, but it begged to be scaled nonetheless. So, as the sun was rising I topped the pile's crest to greet it. There I encountered an interesting collection of animals. In addition to the vultures there were small, sleek dingo dogs and mangy, ragged cats.

I got a clue as to why it is a gathering point for scavengers and carrion eaters when I found rotted and picked over remains of dead animals littering the top and sides of the mound. Where they came from and why there were so many is a mystery I never solved.

Despite the macabre scene, I was drawn back day after day, morning and evening, for from the mound's top I had a great view of one of the narrow, rutty alleyways that ran next to the Heme. I could peek into the courtyards of nearby hovels and eavesdrop on the everyday private life of the Heme's neighbors.

Inside one courtyard, complete with grazing animals, a handful of children played a distant game of hide and seek with me. They darted behind the line of irregular stalks that made up the outside wall of their domicile and back out into plain sight again shouting and waving to me, breaking into screeching laughter when I waved and called back.

In the courtyard next door two women looked up at me from where they sat on their tiny front stoop sifting grain on wide, circular mats, in the same way it has no doubt been done here for thousands of years. I smiled and waved and was delighted when they waved back.

***

After breakfast, we again boarded the shuttle buses for the day's mission— attending church and officially opening ICA's clinic in Angacha.

I was thrilled to see that the newly paved road that connected Addis Ababa to Hossana was being continued past the little town and in the direction we seemed to be headed.

My relief was short-lived. Only a mile or two down the new road we found it blocked off and were informed that, while it looked complete, it wasn't open yet. We had to detour which, to my alarm, meant heading down the nearest embankment and onto what looked to me to be just a sandy cart path disappearing into the African wilds. I soon discovered that this was not just an ordinary cart path but, in fact, a well traveled route.

Though this stretch of road was, in my rather sheltered view, a seriously remote area it was teeming with people, in steady streams walking to and fro about the land. There were women on their way to market and a few elderly men. But mostly, it was children on their way to school or herding a variety of animals: donkeys laden with long poles of sugar cane, scrawny gray cows with camel-like humps behind their heads, or small, shaggy lambs and wiry, nimble goats.

In the dry season, this single-lane trail is a source of thick, choking dust that becomes a blinding cloud when kicked up by vehicles. In the wet, it becomes an impassible quagmire that halts traffic altogether. We were there in what was proving to be an extraordinarily dry season.

A few miles up the trail, the trees parted and we came to a section of the road to Angacha that I came to call the "Ethiopian Super 8." No less than eight different lanes crisscross this huge expanse of grassland.

When vehicles reached this spot, the race was on to be the first across to the next tree lined leg so as to be at the head of the line and not eating someone else's dust. Our driver even managed it once or twice though bruised tailbones were all we had to show for his heroic efforts.

***

We arrived at the village of Angacha that first day to find a large crowd gathered, waiting for us. A dozen or more brightly robed choir members, complete with long cylindrical drums, went ahead of our vehicles, dancing and singing all the way to the church. It seemed as if everyone in the village had turned out and lined the streets to welcome us.

We finally stopped outside a white walled compound. From the outside the church was much like one you might find in rural America. Inside, however, the difference was vast. The walls were made dark by a veneer of black mud intended to insulate against the equatorial heat. There was no glass in the tall window apertures, only colorful curtains, silken panes that mimicked stained glass.

The structure was much longer than it was wide and filled with row upon row of backless wooden benches all packed to overflowing with hundreds of worshippers.

I was surprised to see electric lights suspended from the vaulted girder framework of the ceiling. There were also microphones and a keyboard. It was amazing how much in stride these people took the lapses of electricity that came with maddening regularity throughout the service. In an American church, such frequent, protracted power outages would bring our electronically enhanced services to a quiet and unassuming end. For the Ethiopians it is nothing to be alarmed about; a privilege when present, hardly missed when not.

After a lively service we melded with the crowd surging into the small front yard of the church. Wading through the press, I somehow became separated from my companions. I felt a mixture of frustration and fear as I was swallowed in an ebony sea. A seemingly impenetrable wall of bodies came between me and the familiar sanctuary of my bus. I knew I needed to get through but I didn't know how without elbowing my way and possibly committing some breech of etiquette, or worse, hurting them somehow.

The prickling tingle of tears was just beginning to sting the backs of my eyes when, to my intense relief, Pat Bradley appeared at my side. It wasn't the first time in our years-long friendship that he has come to my rescue and I was more grateful than usual for his timely intervention.

I could only gape, awestruck, when he turned and began wading confidently through the crowd. The dark waters parted easily before him and I followed meekly in his wake.

"You don't need to be afraid," he assured as we went. "These people will never hurt you."

I can't explain why but that was exactly what I needed to hear and it proved the turning point of my trip. At that moment I stopped merely surviving and started experiencing, doing what I had come for: studying the people and their lives in an attempt to document their circumstance.

***

The opening of the clinic, the first fully equipped and professionally staffed medical facility of its kind in this area, was a most auspicious occasion and would not have been complete without a grand ceremony.

We, like guests of honor, were seated apart under a pitched canopy in front of a very large open-air tent that serves as Angacha's high school. This day, however, the rows of benches and desks were not filled with eager students but with elders and local dignitaries wanting to honor Pat and celebrate the achievement.

There were speeches and presentations as with any such landmark celebration. When these were done, the ceremony broke into a procession to the clinic, only a short hike away, for the ribbon cutting portion.

Fighting yet another large crowd that had gathered outside the clinic's fence, we stepped through a narrow wrought iron gate into a beautifully landscaped compound housing an impressive complex of a dozen buildings of varying size and purpose, their fresh paint gleaming brightly in the noonday sun. Only two years before, when the first ICA clinic was conducted on this spot, this was an open field with a couple of dilapidated shacks. The transformation is truly amazing and lends an aura of the miraculous to the place.

After the ribbon-cutting, we boarded the buses again and were taken to a house in the village where members of the church had laid out a celebration feast. While the fare was colorful and looked appetizing enough, I was still not fully recovered from my travels and eating, especially something that could possibly make me violently ill, was pretty much last on my list of "Things to do while in Ethiopia."

I holed up in a corner, still trying to get my bearings and find that elusive level ground on which I could stand confidently. It was while watching the celebrants eat and interact that I began to realize just how charming and delightful the Ethiopian people are.

***

Snapping out of my musings, I glance at the clock on the mantle and see that more than three hours have passed since I got up. It is almost time for me to wake my kids for school and get myself ready for work.

As I stand in the shower just appreciating the warm, clean water, I take inventory and realize that I am sick. Oddly, I am grateful for it. What is most likely a passing discomfort for me is stark and revealing insight into what my Ethiopian brothers and sisters know in some form or fashion virtually every day of their lives. For them, disease is not an occasional visitor but an unwanted resident.

Contemplating this I am taken back to the clinic, the main purpose of our mission. In my mind's eye I see the dark blue canvas of the triage tents set up near the gate, breathe in the mountain fresh air, hear the low din of a hundred murmured conversations, and feel the sun beating relentlessly down upon my head.

The clinic is an island, a masterfully conducted example of order in the midst of chaos. Outside the fence hundreds gathered and local authorities were brought in to keep the ragged crowd in check but, as Pat asserted at the church, none intend violence of any kind. They are sick and hungry and all want to be seen by the first Western-trained medical professionals they have ever come across.

Tragically, because there aren't enough resources only a fraction is admitted, women and children only for this mission. They mob the gate whenever it is opened and surround anyone who comes outside the compound, their plucking hands and eager eyes begging for help.

To our dismay we heard rumors that several who came to the clinic for life sustaining support went right back and sold it to other members of the village who weren't able to get in.

In the "real world" that would be illegal black market activity but in this world where only the fittest survive, the rules seem to be different. I have to ask myself if it is really so bad that someone else has a chance at life where no chance had existed before that morning?

Black merges with white to become ambiguous shades of gray as the lines of right and wrong are blurred by the most basic of instincts— the will to survive. I find that it is hard for me to know how to feel about things in Ethiopia, a land of difficult choices.

One of our buses eating the dust of a construction truck on the road to Angacha.

The "Ethiopian Super 8". The small dust clouds are vehicles racing along the different lanes.

Oncoming traffic would leave us sitting in a blinding cloud of dust.

Everyone always seemed to be going somewhere.

Brightly dressed choir members went before us dancing and singing.

Inside the church.

The ceremony at Angacha's high school. Local dignitaries and government guards were on hand to keep order. Our group was seated under the yellow canopy at the far left.

The procession to the clinic for the ribbon cutting ceremony.

The clinic site in 2006 on ICA's first mission to the area.

The newly completed clinic in February, 2008.

The beautiful landscaping makes the clinic compound a peaceful haven.

A feeding center was added in the summer of 2008. It is estimated that more than 6 million Ethiopians will face starvation in 2009, more than 1 million of which are children under the age of 5.

ICA President, Pat Bradley, being welcomed inside the clinic compound by some grateful friends. These twin babies had been only days from death when they were added to ICA's feeding program.

The feast put together by church members.

Monday . . .

Dressed for the day, the frenzy of the morning's preparations are in full swing around me. I marvel that everything seems so familiar and normal, as if I had never been gone. The moment takes on surreal overtones as I realize that just one week ago I was literally half a world away.

I gaze pensively out the picture window in the dining room at the dawn's magenta halo above the housetops across the street and recall welcoming the scorching Ethiopian sun as it begins its daily dominance of a cerulean sky that seems to stretch forever above rolling hills and sprawling savannah. How quickly it chased away the night's chill.

Shaking off the eerie feeling my thoughts turn to the next logical step in my morning—breakfast. I know I should eat something but my stomach is still somewhere over the Atlantic. I grimace and shudder at the memory of last Monday's breakfast, my first encounter with the Ethiopian idea of breakfast.

Before beginning the trek to Angacha the first morning of the clinic we stopped at a mission hostel to pick up the Ethiopian nurses. They were still eating breakfast so invited us in, and being generous hosts, offered to share their meal with us.

To look at it or even smell it, with its small gristly chunks and heavy spices, I would have thought it sausage with pieces of casing still tightly constricting the pieces rather than the saucy brew of sautéed goat stomach and intestine that it was.

As I was still on a fanatic quest to avoid food and water borne illnesses, I declined as graciously as I could. So as not to offend my new Ethiopian friends, I employed the evasion tactic I had learned the previous day; saying I'm VERY full. It was a struggle to keep a neutral expression and my dehydrated breakfast bar down as I watched them, with fingers and hunks of yellow, cakelike bread, sop up the meaty chunks and rich dark brown gravy.

Little did I know, this was not my last encounter with Ethiopian breakfast.

I started that first morning at the clinic in the pharmacy packing vitamins into pouches. Things were going smoothly and I was starting to feel pretty good about it all when one of the Ethiopian nurses became ill. Unfortunately, she chose the bathroom in the Pharmacy to do it in—right behind where I was sitting.

We all have an Achilles heel or two, something that will reduce us to quivering heaps or have us running for cover every time. Mine is smells. The revisited and enhanced aroma of goat entrails coming from the bathroom had me dashing for the fresh outdoors gagging as I went.

Amazingly, the incident turned out to be a blessing in disguise. Unable to stay in the same room with the lingering smell without vomiting myself, I was reassigned as a runner for the triage area which was a much better fit.

***

An hour later I drop my daughter at her middle school and watch as she eagerly merges into the stream of teens heading into the building, chatting and laughing with several of her friends. It reminds me of the hordes of children who waited outside the gates of the Heme for us. I felt like a celebrity, mobbed by adoring fans as I came out every chance I got to see them. They did not know me the first day but were not daunted. There were so many probing questions.

"What is your name?"

"What is your father's name?"

"What is your grandfather's name?"

"Do you have brothers?"

"Do you have children?"

And on and on it went.

From early in the morning until late at night they called to us, reaching through the bars of the back gate near the room where we took our meals, pleading with us to come over and see them. Pilfered flowers, both real and plastic, were offered up as gifts.

When they saw we were leaving for the day's work they raced back up the street to the front gate where they waved and cheered us out, running alongside the buses until we got to the end of the block. When we returned at the end of the day they were still about, waiting with eager hugs and kisses.

Their persistence stemmed largely from the hope that we would grace them with some gift from America. Most of us had something for them, of course, but the giving must be done carefully in a controlled setting to avoid a riot.

"I love you!" they cried over and over.

I cannot help but love them back.

The children waiting at the gate of the Heme for us to come out.

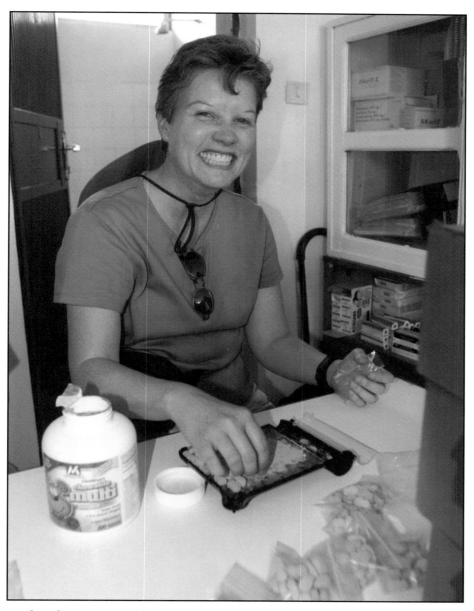

In the pharmacy packing vitamins. Directly behind me is the bathroom.

Hundreds gather outside the clinic gate hoping to be seen. More than 1,000 were treated over the three days of our clinic.

Women and children patiently waiting their turn.

The triage area set up near the front entrance of the clinic compound.

"Aund-so!"

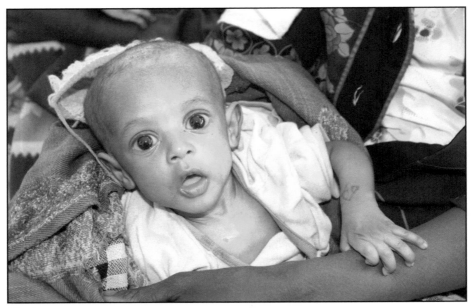

Curious eyes.

Pat and his wife, Sue, with severly malnourished twins. Their mother can't produce enough milk to feed them because she, too, is malnourished.

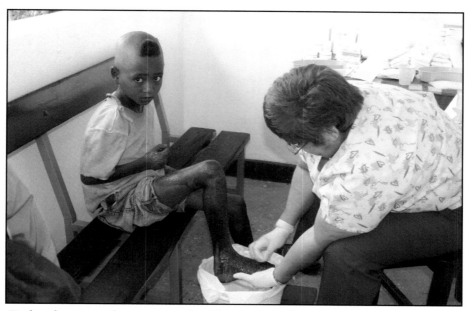

Carla, the wound care specialist, brings comfort and healing to a young patient.

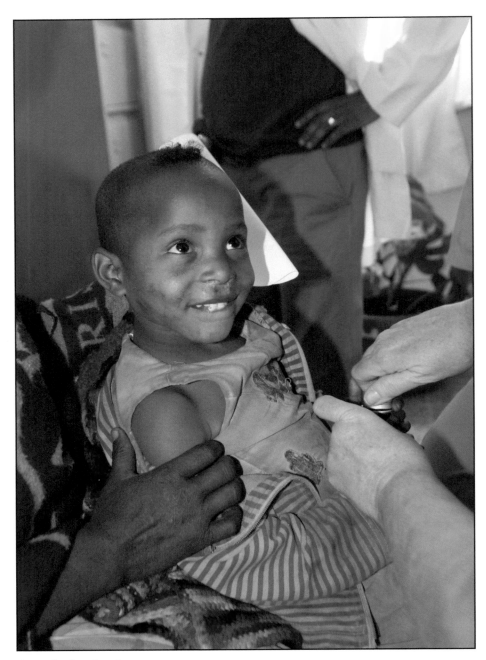

A smile for the doctor.

Special delivery – bags of grain for the feeding program are brought to the clinic by donkey cart.

This baby has hope for the future because of ICA's work.

Tuesday . . .

As I rest my tired eyes midmorning, other parts of my visit to Ethiopia scroll across my memory. I recall the afternoon of the second day of the clinic when I got to go out into the countryside with Pat and his team for the feeding program.

Our little group, packed into SUV's, left Angacha and stopped a half hour later at a bend in the track, where stood a small cluster of buildings and huts next to which was a crudely fashioned corral of twisted sticks driven into the ground and held together by the fronds of whatever bush or tree provides such things. Within the enclosure were several tin and mud brick structures. This is where we would be setting up the feeding program and clinic that afternoon.

While preparations were being made by the medical and ICA staff, I took the opportunity to look around. Hopping up onto the thigh-high concrete wall casing running along the back of the enclosure, I discovered it to be a small canal filled with gray-green water upon which floated an oily crust of stagnation.

As I followed the water course around the backside of the hill I was afforded a marvelous view of rolling brown fields dotted with scrubby, flat-topped trees adjoining other fields and hills which adjoined still more fields and hills. On and on they rolled as far as I could see.

The little kid in me wanted to go exploring, to see what was beyond that farthest hill, though I suspected the scenery from there would be very similar to what I was looking at now. I was certain this was the "wanderlust" every explorer who ever was must have felt when surveying a new land.

With a sigh I turned back to the compound and the tasks waiting for me. That was when I noticed the small knot of children gathered beside the canal to watch me. They followed as I began walking again. One brave young man even jumped up on the canal wall near me. I was delighted when he met my eyes and we shared a smile.

My pleasure faded when, beyond him, I saw another boy scooping the foul water from the canal into his palm for a drink. Water, either the lack or quality of it, remains at the heart of Ethiopia's struggles and a big part of what has brought us here this day.

By the time I made my way back, a large, hopeful crowd had gathered around the corral fence. I'm not sure where they came from but I knew why they were there. They are starving and know Pat has brought food and medicine.

What they didn't know is that we didn't have very much of either, certainly not enough for everyone. As at the clinic, most gathered around the fence would go home empty handed. Again, only mothers with infants had priority.

They were admitted in groups of seven and seated in spots around the corral. A small plastic band was slipped around each infant's arm to assess the MUAC (Middle-Upper Arm Circumference) which measures the degree of malnutrition. The lower the number, the closer they are to dying. Any circumference under 12.5 centimeters is considered severe.

While the fortunate were receiving food and medical treatment in one of the tin buildings, I was doing the only thing I was qualified to do here—crowd control. I was handed a big stick and given a corner of the compound to police, a job that proved harder than I imagined.

The press of the crowd against the fence constantly threatened to push it over so the people had to be kept from leaning on it. I soon discovered that wasn't the only problem when suddenly a small boy, perhaps three or four years old, wriggled between the legs of the onlookers and shot into the corral from beneath the lowest cross-timber.

A look of terror crossed his face as I instantly dodged right to head him off. He immediately changed direction to avoid me. There was a comic quality to the scene that wasn't lost on me. Although I was horrified by his reaction, I was reminded of the greased pig contest at the rodeo as, to the twitters of the crowd, I dodged this way and that to head the boy off.

Seeing he wouldn't get past me without risking physical contact he apparently decided discretion was the better part of valor and hotfooted it back out the way he had come, not stopping until he was a good distance away. He stood for a moment glowering at me before wandering off.

I was further dismayed to see the same look of fear and suspicion mirrored in many of the faces peeking through the fence. Something in me insisted that I needed to bridge the gap, show them I meant them no harm. If nothing else make them smile. If we couldn't send them away with food, perhaps I could send them away with a kinder idea of westerners.

It would have been the perfect time for a story but none of them spoke English so I moved to the universal language of mime. They seemed to find my stick balancing and rousing game of invisible baseball amusing enough but that got old pretty quickly. Then, digging deep into my long ago, I pulled out an old favorite—The Hokey Pokey.

I never imagined it would be such a hit. Over and over I put my parts in and out and toward the end even enticed a few to play along. Justin, a young member of our group, also set to guarding the fence, commented that they'd probably be talking (and maybe even laughing) about "that crazy white woman" for years to come.

Finally, heat wore me down and I could Pokey no more so I plopped against the wall of the nearest building to rest and the crowd settled in to watch me do it. Vigorously fanning my face with my bush hat, I finished my bottle of water and was about to stuff the empty into my backpack to dispose of properly later when I noticed hands stretching through the fence toward me.

Holding up the empty bottle I quickly deduced that they wanted it. It was in that moment that I truly understood how precious resources were to these people, particularly water and anything useful in holding it. Unable to think of any fair way to give away this treasure I cocked my arm and threw it as far over the fence as I could.

Most of the pack took off after it and a melee ensued until finally someone succeeded in securing the precious empty. Seeing nothing else of real interest developing, the bulk of the crowd wandered off.

Running out of food, medicine, and daylight our time there was quickly winding to its end. With little left to do but wait, I had a last look around.

Across the road from the corral was the only green grass around. It was a strip framing an ambling trace that must be the local source of running water. I glanced left, up the road a little ways, and saw a donkey standing in the middle of the tiny stream. To my right a dozen or so feet, were women and children drinking and washing in the same water in which the animal had just urinated.

It was inconceivable to me that they didn't recognize the potential health risks of that situation, but then I recalled that their beasts of burden are highly prized possessions that even stay in the huts with the family to ensure the animal's safety.

I am tempted to call it primitive ignorance but that would be selling these people far short. Perhaps I, with my western education and "higher" standards of sanitation, would proclaim it such, but then I must understand that these people are only doing the best they can with what they've got. As a testimony to survival at its fittest, they have been doing so for eons. I suppose if I had one donkey to plow my little field and haul me and my goods about or a single goat to give milk for my children and sell to my neighbors as a source of income, and the loss would mean losing the battle to subsist, I might treat it as a family member as well.

Only then did I truly see how enormous the gap is between my technology driven Western world and the survival driven Ethiopian world where life is at its simplistic best. I cannot help but wonder who's really the more disadvantaged here.

Emotionally and physically drained by the intensive afternoon, we piled back into our vehicles and began the long drive back to Hossana and the Heme where a much appreciated shower and meal were waiting. I felt a twinge of guilt for thinking this charming bastion of protection and convenience was a serious step down. A mere forty-eight hours after my initial disdain it had become a haven of coveted luxuries for which I was most grateful.

During the arduous drive back, I looked out at the now-familiar scenery, made golden by the setting sun, and ruminated on how marvelous it is that I can just pop in to visit blessings upon their world, leave them with a little food and The Hokey Pokey, and pop back out to my own world of comfort and luxury. It began to dawn on me that, although I came here to make a positive impact on their world, it was they who were impacting mine.

A typical rural homestead. Many of these dot the hills around Angacha.

This goat shares tight quarters with the rest of the family.

Inside the small, circular huts, the occupants must make the best of the space.

The family kitchen.

The view from the backside of where we conducted the feeding program.

Beyond the next hill.

Me in my corner practicing "Big Stick Diplomacy". Justin (right) minds the gate.

Peeking through the corral slats. The boy in orange at the bottom was the subject of my 'greased pig' episode.

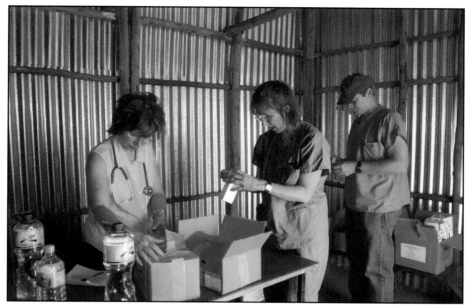

The medical staff sets up shop in one of the tin buildings.

Each baby is checked for signs of malnutrition.

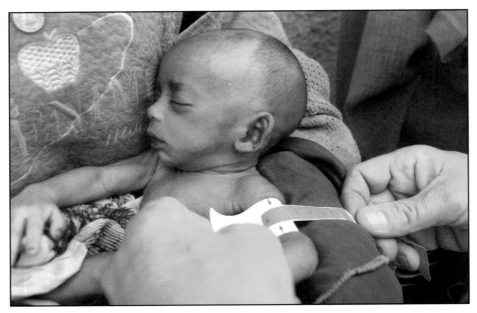

The MUAC (Middle-Upper Arm Circumference) is used to determine level of malnutrition. Anything under 12.5 centimeters is considered severe. This baby measured just above 6 centimeters.

Across the road from the corral, this trace is a popular spot for people and animals alike (note the numerous piles of animal waste in and around the stream).

There was a donkey standing in the water a dozen feet upstream from where this boy was drinking.

Wednesday . . .

The morning is passing strangely unnoticed while I sit at the kitchen table contemplating the eternal question that has vexed wives and mothers since the dawn of time: "What's for dinner?"

I feel I should tackle the problem early in the day since a shopping trip is needed. Unfortunately, my appetite still hasn't recovered and I fear I will do little more than sit at the table with my family poking unenthusiastically at whatever ends up on my plate.

A smile tugs at my lips. I was puzzled when I found "a can of Spam with no questions" on the list of requirements for the trip. That's right, Spam. It wasn't until our last night in Hossana that those of us new to the mission found out what it was for. The dentist in our group produced several boxes of Zatarain's Red Beans and Rice and, taking the Spam each of us had brought, disappeared into the Heme's kitchen to produce a true feast.

I never imagined Spam could taste so wonderful though I suspect five days of granola bars, protein paste, and dried fruit had a little something to do with it.

Maki the Manager, further delighted us by arranging for a woman to perform the traditional Ethiopian coffee ceremony. The meal was wonderful, the company grand. We were all tired but reveled in the relief of having successfully accomplished the mission. We could go home satisfied. Unfortunately for me, that was to prove short lived.

You see, before the trip began there were three things that occupied that horrifying place of "worst nightmare" for me: getting bumped and missing international connections (which happened but we survived), the polluted air aggravating my asthma (which was happening but I was surviving) and getting a food/water borne illness (which I was lucky enough to avoid so far).

As "Spam Night" drew to a close, the last worst happened—I came down with an intestinal malady. It hit so suddenly, without any warning whatsoever, I could do nothing but sprint up the stairs to my room. Just as suddenly, I went from tired but happy to so weak and dizzy I was unable to stand or even crawl from the bathroom to my bed.

Thankfully, my roommate found me propped against the wall near the bathroom and went for help. Within moments a bevy of well-seasoned doctors and nurses blessed me with their knowledge and all the antibiotics, anti-diarrheals, and nutrient replenishers needed to put me back together enough for the trip back to Addis Ababa the next day.

I never fully understood before that night how thoroughly devastating such illness can be, how something so seemingly minor can decimate whole populations. Sure, I'd been sick before but never anything like this.

For this, as every other aspect of the trip, I could be thankful since the experience gave me a whole new perspective on my life. For the first time, I really understood on every level how privileged I am to have water and food I can safely consume. I never imagined how taxing it could be to painstakingly monitor every single thing I came in contact with. Not a single aspect of my life could be overlooked. I had been so very careful I'm still not sure how I contracted that nasty little bug.

That evening marked a second turning point in the trip for me—I was ready to go home and be a spoiled American again.

***

Now, a handful of days later, I am back where I belong and surrounded by all my things. Yet I'm at a loss as to where to start, how to get my life going again.

At my desk for the first time in two weeks, I scan the dark oak surface. It is almost completely covered by the clutter of my industry: stacks of books and magazines, baskets full of work done and to be done, Thesauruses, dictionaries and the laptop on its stand. Beyond are worktables for creating dolls, jewelry, paper treasures and paintings. Lining the walls are rows and rows of shelves packed with the supplies that fuel my little arts business.

As I lean back in my chair, taking in all I have, I am reminded of those who have so much less, not nearly enough to do the jobs they've been given to do.

I remember Woldekidan Arficho and Johannes Workneh, the English teachers, who acted as translators during the days at the clinic. Having also been a teacher once I felt an instant bond with them, particularly Woldekidan who teaches seventh grade.

I was surprised to learn that he wasn't always a teacher. Once he was studying to be a priest. He shared wistfully of how he has a teaching certificate but dreams of going to University in Addis Ababa to earn a degree so he can go from making sixty dollars a month to ninety-five.

I cannot help but smile again as I recall how these two would beckon to me to send the next patient to one of the three triage tents:

"'J' one more!" they would call.

I would then turn to the line of patiently waiting women and children and say, "Aund-so," the word for *one more*. And one family group would come forward.

My new Ethiopian friends, including the government guards posted about to keep order, would laugh appreciatively.

The teachers, Johannes and Woldekidan, would beam and say proudly, "I taught her that."

Just now I reach for the pen lying close at hand, ready to write a note to myself and my smile fades. How can I have so much I take for granted?

I close my eyes, momentarily overcome, and am surrounded by them again; the children of affliction, malnutrition stamped across their skeletal features, dark eyes glazed and protuberant, heads lolling listlessly, mouths slack. A mother of starving twins holds up her breasts shaking her head. She has no milk to give for she, too, is starving.

I see the bent and broken old woman, sad eyes pleading as she pats her belly then makes gestures toward her mouth. She is hungry but because of our limited resources we are not there to feed her, only babies and nursing mothers in the most desperate shape. It was with deep regret that I sent her toward the exit gate and back into the street. She bowed her head, resigned, and left the clinic compound but not my thoughts. I cannot help but wonder if she is still alive today.

Shaking off the troubling images, I open my eyes with renewed determination to get something constructive done. The recent pictures of my two children on the desk in front of me catches my eye. I notice, as if for the first time, how beautiful and grown up my thirteen-year-old daughter is looking. Of a sudden I am once again looking into the beautiful, angelic face of a tiny girl. I'm sadly certain I didn't hide my shock when her mother said that she was thirteen. I could have sworn she was no more than five or six.

The removal of the girl's wraps and tunic revealed a grotesque hump of spinal deformity, that and her stunted size painfully obvious signs of lifelong malnutrition. Her mother confirmed that she stopped growing years ago. This girl and her bleak prospects for the future impacted me more deeply than any of the others.

Meeting her mother's doleful eyes I felt her heartache as if it were a physical torment inside me. This mother wants no less for her daughter than I want for mine. My beautiful daughter will be able to achieve many of her hopes and dreams while her Ethiopian counterpart, even graced with a beautiful face, can't afford hopes and dreams for they will only be disappointed. My heart still breaks for them both.

And so I learned that Ethiopia is a land of stark and heartbreaking contrasts.

"Spam Night" at the Heme.

The traditional coffee ceremony.

A traditional Ethiopian coffee pot.

An honest to goodness third-world toilet.

The English teacher, Woldekidan Arficho.

The English teacher, Johannes Workneh (center) acts as translator in one of the triange tents.

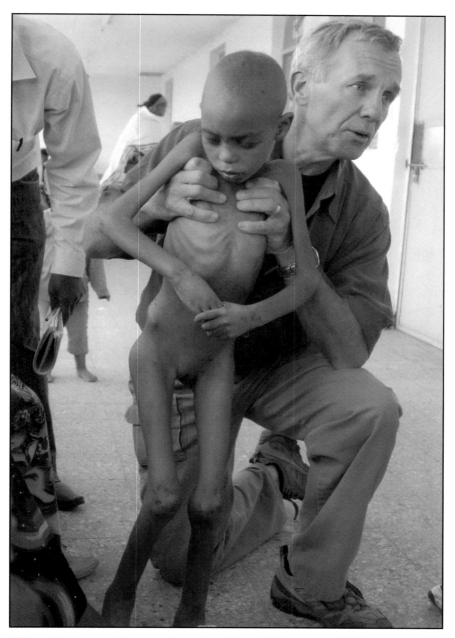

This girl is one of more than 1 million Ethiopian children currently facing starvation.

Thursday . . .

Watching my son amidst the joyful hordes of just released children dash across the playground of his elementary school to where I sit waiting to pick him up at the end of his day, I am reminded of the orphanage complex ICA is building on the outskirts of Addis Ababa where we stopped on the way back from Hossana.

The first building, though still under construction at the time, was taking shape. It is to be home to girls who have been orphaned by HIV/AIDS and have nowhere else to go but the streets. Pat has a great vision for this place. He dreams of building a whole thriving complex complete with a school.

Standing in the desolate field behind the construction site, I turned my eyes to the hills rising to peak. Up the long, lumpy slopes I saw small knots of sheep, goats, and cattle lazily grazing. It struck me as something like a scene from the Ethiopian version of *The Sound of Music* and I felt serenity there. It is a place of sanctuary where peace, like cool, refreshing water, flows through the soul.

There was a hut on the far boundary to my right and a curious girl watched us from the fence. I was drawn to her, wondering if she had ever spoken to a "crazy white woman" before. Within moments we were joined by another teen. She was wearing a shirt with English words on it.

"Love," I read for her pointing to the word but she shook her head, not understanding.

Since they did not speak English we got little more communicated besides our names. Still I felt good for having tried.

I started back to the group, hopping over the shallow gullies and ravines that scar the sparsely vegetated plot of land, and tried to picture this place as Pat envisions it, a thriving campus beautifully landscaped, teeming with hundreds of girls, bright futures in the making.

I left that place feeling more hopeful and lighter of spirit than I had in days.

After seeing the orphanage, we checked into the Hilton and settled down in the lap of luxury (even by American standards) to rest for a few hours before the next part of the mission. Although still under the weather, I eagerly anticipated the coming night. That evening, our last in-country, would be "The Banquet," a feast vastly different from the previous evening's "Spam Night" at the Heme. This night was an elaborate celebration for the American and Ethiopian participants of the mission.

The sun was riding low as we were driven across Addis Ababa to a surprisingly elegant restaurant. As on my first day in-country, I found myself lounging on a tall hill overlooking the sprawling city. As night fell, orange lights winked on but not in the densely organized way as in American cities. The lights here were liberally scattered, with many pockets of darkness.

The evening was a time of fellowship and sharing and concluded with what was hands down the highlight of the trip for me—getting to present the gifts I had brought to Pat's "Ethiopian daughters," as he calls the girl's he has rescued from sex slavery.

Not surprisingly, emotionally and physically exhausted as I was, I ended the trip much as it had begun, with a mini-meltdown. Pat, more mentor and big brother to me than just a friend, in true brotherly fashion strongly counseled that I must learn to control my emotions else this work would eat me alive.

You see, he knew that I had dreamed of taking such a trip as this for more than a decade and even dreamed of doing such work as his full time but now I know that is not my calling. I am not strong enough.

I know now that I am called only to *chronicle* the life and death struggles and share them with you, the empowered reader, the one who can actually *make* the difference between life and death in Ethiopia—a place of harsh realties.

The orphanage under construction in February 2008.

The completed orphanage in February 2009.

In their new home. Because of ICA these girls are no longer faced with living in the streets.

The view from the back door of the orphanage. Despite the desolate appearance there is peace here.

Addis Ababa as seen from the restaurant where we had "The Banquet".

Pat's "Ethiopian Daughters". Just a few of the dozens of girls ICA has rescued from sex slavery.

Getting to present the gifts I had brought to the girls. The highlight of the trip for me!

The American and Ethiopian participants of the mission enjoy some fellowship as the evening winds to a close.

Friday . . .

It is well past bedtime in my world that was but only late afternoon in my now. Completely exhausted but still with hours left in my day, I close my eyes for a short nap and again see the multitudes lining the smooth, paved streets of Addis Ababa.

Sitting, lying, walking; they are the vast and thriving subculture that is a street-dwelling homeless population of staggering proportions. Most seem to be going nowhere in particular, the sum of their existence being in the place along the curb where they stop.

By contrast to the dusty savannah byways of the country, the streets of the capital are filthy and chaotic, choked by litter and ditches filled with everything from dirty dishwater to human waste.

It seems strange to me that the city folk tend to look down upon their rural brothers, as if the simple life of the latter is of lesser stature than the "sophisticated" backwater of the city.

A gasp of horror escaped my lips as, on our way to one of the homes ICA has started for girls redeemed from sex slavery, we sped by a mother reclining against a wall only a few feet from the street, her baby visibly sick, was obviously dying.

"Don't look at it," came Pat's gentle counsel in my ear. "Keep your eyes straight ahead."

Sage advice from a well seasoned veteran of the mission field with service in more than thirty-five countries. I long to heed it but I cannot. I must look. I must report what I see to you, the inquisitive reader. If you do not know, you cannot care and if you, who can make a difference, do not care then there is no hope.

My dismay grew as I continued to look at the people flashing past the car window. I spotted tiny shelters along the route, doghouse-sized boxes fashioned out of a few pieces of corrugated tin, hardly big enough for a small child to curl up in. As cramped as they may be, the owners of these little boxes seem to be the lucky ones for they have a roof, some protection. So many others have nothing but a few ragged shreds of cloth to protect them from the hard ground and cool nights.

More than one lay prostrate, contorted, unmoving—dead. The fate that awaits us all eventually has come sooner to these victims of an unsuccessful attempt to eek out an existence in a harsh and unforgiving land. I can't help but wonder what their last thoughts must have been, caught up as they were in the unimaginable tragedy of dying alone on the street, the epitome of hopelessness.

We stopped for a red light and were instantly assailed by professional beggars, all children. These junior hustlers deftly darted and weaved through the rows of waiting vehicles to stop at every window and make their pitch.

"Money, money, money!" they chanted, hands outstretched.

This time I did heed Pat's advice and fixed my eyes straight ahead for I had nothing to give them. Seeing my lack of attention they quickly moved on and in another few moments, so did we.

We turned into a narrow alley and bumped down a steep cobbled lane. As we slowed to a stop at our destination, I found myself looking down at a woman washing dishes in front of a long section of corrugated tin sheets. I watched in disgusted fascination as she dipped a dish into murky brown water in a beat up tin basin at the far left, then into brownish-gray water in the center basin where she used a ragged strip of brown cloth to work up an anemic lather, then into the grayish-brown water in the basin at far right. Deemed "clean," the dish, which had clearly seen better days, was set aside, ready for the next meal.

I had to remind myself that it wasn't yet another ruthless assault on everything I knew about sanitation, it was the best she could do with what she has.

***

Later, as I waited in the lane outside the walls of the girls' home for my companions to conclude their business, an old woman, skin like crumpled brown paper spread across the bones of a face that has long ago forgotten how to smile, hobbled over to dump urine from an old paint can into the ditch beside me. She spoke to me conversationally but I could only shake my head and shrug helplessly, the barrier of language keeping us forever strangers. With a shrug she shuffled back to her tiny shack, a corner made home by a little corrugated tin.

My eyes wondered around the rough cul-de-sac sloping away past the old woman's corner, the afterthought of a street that dead-ended in the back of a large concrete building.

As I strolled the short distance down the hill toward the dead-end, I noticed more tin shacks in other angles where buildings came together. To my left was a small recess filled with two tiny hovels between which was a young woman with a toddler and an old woman beside her going about the chores of the day. They stopped only for a moment to give me smiling glances then went back to their work.

Looking away, my gaze following the line of a long fence stretching to the right of the building in front of me, I was surprised to find an entire tin shed subdivision in two neat rows lining another steeply sloped and deeply eroded alley.

Shortly, a young teenage girl approached me from one of the shacks to my left with a purple rubber ball. She didn't speak English either but through gestures communicated that she would like me to play ball with her. At first I thought she meant volley ball but then she walked to a narrow section of the dead end wall and stopped between two poles a dozen feet apart. She gestured with her foot for me to kick it. I gathered then that she meant soccer instead and wanted to practice her skills as goalie with me as the scorer.

Soon our game was interrupted by the toddler who took the ball and ran with it. I saw regret in the girl's eyes as she followed the little boy who must have been a relative, part of the family with whom she resides in one of those tiny sheds.

It occurred to me to wonder why she wasn't in school, whether she was one of the roughly 70 percent of Ethiopian children who can't afford to go to school. Sadly, she looks to be a prime candidate for why Pat has started the girls' homes and built the orphanage.

As a parent my heart ached for the girl and all the others in this slum area for they stand the sad chance of ending up on the streets.

Poverty here can be so severe that there seems to be no other choice for parents than to send the children off to work wherever and at whatever is available to them. Others are forced into the streets because both parents have succumbed to disease and leave them nowhere else to go.

However they end up there, the girls in particular become prey to sex slavers who offer them what looks to be legitimate money making opportunities. Once entrapped, the girls, some as young as four years old, become slaves locked in hovels hardly bigger than the size of the cot or mat on which they sleep, more like cages than rooms because they cannot leave. Their lives become a living hell as, every night, they are forced to sexually service as many adult male clients as possible, sometimes a dozen or more.

By their mid-teen years many have contracted venereal diseases, including HIV/AIDS, and given birth to children, who stand a better than average chance of perpetuating the tragic cycle.

On every visit possible, Pat makes a trip to the "Red Light" district looking for likely girls to rescue. His reputation is beginning to grow and word of his purpose starting to spread. Each time he goes to the district now, by the time he leaves with his newest "Ethiopian daughter," others have gathered their few belongings and come to him, begging to go too. It breaks his heart but he must turn them away because there is nowhere to put them—yet anyway.

Pat will be back for them. It is a silent promise he makes to himself and them and keeps praying and working tirelessly to expand the program. I can only pray it is vast and wide enough to protect this girl I have enjoyed a game of soccer with should that prove to be her fate.

As we returned to the Hilton at the end of the last long and busy day of the mission, leaving the tumultuous squalor of the streets for the island of true five-star luxury, the young soldier with an AK-47 across his knees seated in a chair outside the hotel gate brings it all into perspective for me. He is evidence of the true gravity of the daily life and death struggles that go on within Ethiopia, a country peacefully at war with itself because of extreme poverty.

Pat Bradley spends an afternoon with some of his "Ethiopian Daughters".

Looking for another "Ethiopian Daughter".

Bringing help and hope to Addis Ababa's Red Light district.

Pat introduces himself to a girl he hopes to rescue. You can see the conditions in which she lives are less than ideal.

It isn't hard to find someone in need of help.

A tin shanty neighborhood.

Life in these areas is challenging to say the least.

Young boys contribute to the family income by begging in the streets.

Once rescued, the girls are given vocational training so they can earn a living.

Some of the girls have given birth to children.

Sadly, many are forced into sex slavery at a very young age. Newly arrived, this girl hasn't yet found her smile...but it will come in time as it has to the rest of Pat's "Ethiopian Daughters" (some of whom are shown in the following pictures).

Tomorrow . . .

Before bed, at the end of a surprisingly hard first day back home, I slip into the tub for a long, hot bath. I want to be clean again, oblivious in my naïve ignorance with my comfortable "not my problem" attitude. To be free of the burden of knowledge.

But there is no way to go back, to undo what has already been done, to un-see all that's already been seen. I can only go forward from here, toward absolution, in search of a new place of peace.

The only way to undo what is, is to change it. The only way to change it is to become actively involved. To do whatever I can until I no longer see the dying and contend with the knowledge that there must be something I can do to help even just one.

As the warm and comforting water covers my tired, aching body, I reflect on my spoiled state of "American-ness." In retrospect, I see that this trip was not about comfort, but being taken out of my place of comfort, my safety zone where things go as planned, and cast headlong into the freefall of trusting a higher authority, the God I serve, to work it all out when things seem to go very, very wrong.

Is it wrong to be spoiled? I wonder.

Only if it keeps me from making wrongs right or trying to make a real and lasting difference in the world, I decide.

This gives rise to the next logical question: *How can one make a difference in a world so seemingly upside-down?*

Early in the 2003 film *Tears of the Sun,* Bruce Willis's character cynically states that "God already left Africa." For reasons I didn't understand as I watched from the safety of my living room, that scene stuck in my mind. I have revisited and mulled it over from time to time over the years since. Perhaps, down deep all that time I wondered if it really is so. Has God abandoned Africa? Left her to founder and drown in a sea of darkness?

In the opinion of a Nigerian friend, Africa is not dark at all, but rather blessed because there is a much greater opportunity for good there. Light is indeed brighter and more effective at night than during the day.

This trip showed me two important things: 1) God has not left Africa. He is alive and well and working diligently on behalf of His people. And 2) while in need of help, Africa is not in need of anymore quick fixes. She is in need of slow, healing, tender ministrations.

Perhaps it is a continent ravaged by disease, many preventable. Or it is ripped apart by hatred, brutality, and greed but, what if, as poets and optimists believe, love truly can effectively nurture the dying and counter hate? What if little acts of genuine, heartfelt kindness made by people willing to give of their resources or even leave their places of comfort and be uncomfortable for a week or two, can right the worst wrongs?

It is true that during my seven days in Ethiopia, while I developed a "new and improved" definition of discomfort and lost many of my illusions, I found along the road of this adventure something deep inside myself that refuses to be contained in the limitation of human words.

Is it curiosity? A desire to know what makes this indomitable people so indomitable? I don't know, perhaps I never will. What I do know is that they suffer unspeakably, yet their smiles are wide and genuine. They look different and speak a different language, yet now I see that we are not so different as we might like to imagine. We all have hopes, dreams, desired outcomes for our trips, whether it be around the world or down the road to market. Each life, whether here or in Africa, or anywhere else in the world for that matter, is a rich and varicolored tapestry, an amazing picture that cannot be reproduced by anyone else, only experienced and remembered.

***

The day finally behind me, I snuggle between my soft sheets under my downy comforter and am struck by the last comparison of this long, strange day, how I dropped into the small bed at the Heme feeling much the same; exhausted, my emotions raw, completely overwhelmed by the sight of dying children and hopeless people. There I cried. Although I tried to hide the tears at the clinic, one of the interpreters saw them and asked what was wrong. I told him that my heart was breaking for the people. He said that it was good but that the people must not see it. For them I must put on a happy face. For them I must be strong.

In my own bed with no one but God to see, I am free to weep for their misery and bleak future but, despite a heavy heart, I can't. My tears are gone. In their place is resolve, a resolve to share what I've seen and do what I can to help. But that is for tomorrow. For now, I must try to sleep.

I sharply order the specters back to where they came from; the country folk to their small circular huts of mud and thatch scattered in seemingly random fashion throughout the hills, the city dwellers to the cramped square rooms of tin or crumbling mud brick. But they remain with me. I fear they always will, to curse me with their want.

Or is it a gift they've given me? Had I not seen them I would not truly appreciate how blessed I am. I can feed my two children, *my* daughter is tall and beautiful and more worried about what to wear to school than cheating the death and deprivation that relentlessly hunts *them*.

Again I'm confronted by the hopeless eyes of a mother who knows that for her child there is no bright future.

I desperately fight off the anguish that suddenly threatens to pull me under again. Though terrible, this too is a gift I realize, for to see and feel nothing would signal an inexcusable callousness and frightening lack of compassion, cold indifference born of a life of self-indulgence.

I cannot help but wonder how you, the reader, will take what I have shared. Will you become indignant that I would appeal to you for help? We do, after all, have so many problems of our own.

I have heard so many say, "Why should I waste money on a people who lack industry and breed like rabbits? They are only getting what they deserve."

Ashamedly, I must admit that I had even thought it a time or two myself in the past.

Perhaps you have looked at the enormity of the issue and decided it's just too big for one person to fix. You wonder what you can possibly do to make a difference. I know I have been caught in that web as well.

Thanks to Pat Bradley, I went and saw for myself what one convinced and determined person can do. You see, Pat learned of the plight of the Ethiopians in 2003 after reading a news story on the growing famine there. He landed in Addis Ababa a short time later not knowing a soul, with only a phone number in his pocket.

Today, through his tireless efforts to raise support and activate others, he has an adopted Ethiopian family numbering into the thousands and through ICA's work is transforming the barren landscape and giving many of Ethiopia's children a future and hope for it.

I saw for myself that there was nothing to fear, that they are only people, a once mighty people part of Kush, Nubia and Axum. Each was a great empire that ruled much of East Africa and even rated prominent mention in the Christian Bible. They have fallen into disgrace and despair, becoming a nation crippled by need with hands out to receive crumbs and scraps from the great foreign table.

I would assert that it isn't a situation entirely of their own making, that they are not merely "getting what they deserve." Rather, they are victims of circumstances largely beyond their control—the men can't control the weather, that sometimes the rains don't come, or they come too greatly and wash away the crops or make them rot in the ground. The women can't control the fact that they are viewed as lesser and are at the mercy of a male-dominated society. The children can't control the fact that their parents grow sick and die and leave them without shelter or support.

Perhaps the saddest fact of all is that the Ethiopian people have been in the grips of hopelessness for so long they have forgotten what hope is. If they are only getting what they deserve, then how much worse could we, who have control of our destiny and theirs, deserve for seeing their plight and doing nothing or, worse, not caring at all?

I think of young America with our pioneering spirit and our willingness to help a neighbor in need. Are we not all neighbors in this ever shrinking world? The Ethiopian man being consumed by leprosy is no less human and able to feel pain and the devastation of his disease than you or I. Perhaps he, and the rest of his people, feel pain more acutely because they are so intimately acquainted with it. Perhaps they bear their burden so gracefully because they have felt it so long they have become numb to it and simply accept it as an immutable fact of life.

Perhaps, this generation *is* hopeless but the next need not be. With a little help for our sick and dying sister, Ethiopia can become a beacon of hope, a bright light in a very dark place. Call it terminal optimism if you like. I prefer to think of it as a good start on rescuing all of Africa.

It is a grand vision I have. But I realize it is not one I can accomplish on my own. I can only put words to paper and tell you of their suffering. It is you, the now informed, knowledgeable reader, who must take my words and give them substance. You must make them into something real and give them power by joining them to your actions.

Perhaps you have no such vision, are not equipped or even desire to go, but then you don't have to. Perhaps you have a little extra that you can give. Therein lies the real power as it puts resources into the hands of people, like Pat Bradley, who choose and desire to go and meet the Ethiopian people at the place of their need—a place where there is no comfort.

*For more information on **Pat Bradley** and **International Crisis Aid's** work in Ethiopia and around the world go to www.crisisaid.org.*

LaVergne, TN USA
01 December 2010
207067LV00008B